This book shows the growth of an English village from a medieval clearing to the urban congestion of the present day. The village is seen from the same viewpoint approximately every hundred years. The castle, the church, the market cross and the house on the right survive to some extent down the centuries; the interior of the house changes as social patterns change. Rural life in England remained remarkably untouched by outside events (except for their Civil War of 1642) until the advent of the automobile.

THE STORY OF
AN ENGLISH VILLAGE

John S. Goodall

A MARGARET K. McELDERRY BOOK

Atheneum   1979   New York

14th Century

15th
Century

16th
Century

17th
Century

18th
Century